Table of Contents

Introduction..3
Chapter 1: Introduction to Personal Finance.......... 3
Chapter 1: Introduction to Personal Finance.......... 5
Chapter 2: Creating a Personal Budget.................. 9
Chapter 3: Managing Debt and Credit.................. 13
Chapter 4: Understanding the Importance of Saving and Emergency Funds...17
Chapter 5: Investing for the Future....................... 21
Chapter 6: Retirement Planning............................25
Chapter 7: Insurance and Risk Management....... 29
Chapter 8: Tax Planning and Optimization............35
Chapter 9: Estate Planning and Wealth Transfer..39
Chapter 10: Continuously Improving and Monitoring Your Financial Health..44

Introduction

Welcome to "The Ultimate Guide on How To Master Personal Finance!" If you're an entrepreneur looking to gain control over your financial life and set yourself up for long-term success, you've come to the right place.

This book is your all-in-one resource, crafted especially for individuals like you who are eager to navigate the often complex world of personal finance. We're going to dive deep into a wide range of financial topics, from budgeting and saving to investing and planning for retirement.

Our goal is simple: to equip you with the knowledge and strategies you need to make smart, informed decisions about your money. Think of this guide as your trusted companion on your financial journey. Whether you're just starting out or looking to refine your financial skills, we've got you covered.

So, get ready to transform your financial life. Let's embark on this journey together and take the first steps toward a secure and prosperous future.

Chapter 1: Introduction to Personal Finance

Welcome to the exciting journey of personal finance! In this chapter, we'll lay the groundwork for your financial adventure by diving into the fundamental concepts and principles that will guide you along the way. By understanding these basics, you'll gain a clear perspective on how money works and how to manage it effectively.

First, let's talk about income and expenses. Income is the money you earn, whether from a job, investments, or other sources. Expenses, on the other hand, are the costs you incur for living, such as rent, groceries, and entertainment. It's crucial to understand the balance between your income and expenses because this balance determines your financial health.

Next, we'll explore assets and liabilities. Assets are things you own that have value, like your home, car, or savings account. Liabilities are what you owe, such as loans, credit card debt, or mortgages. Knowing the difference between assets and liabilities is essential because it helps you understand your net worth, which is a measure of your financial stability.

One of the key aspects of personal finance is setting financial goals. Why are financial goals so important? They give you a direction and purpose for your money. Whether you're saving for a vacation, buying a home, or planning for retirement, having clear goals will motivate you to stick to your financial plan.

Now, let's discuss the importance of creating a budget. A budget is a plan for your money that outlines your expected income and expenses. By tracking your spending, you can see where your money goes and identify areas where you can cut back if needed. A budget helps you live within your means, avoid debt, and save for future goals.

By the end of this chapter, you'll have a solid understanding of personal finance and be well-prepared to embark on your financial planning journey. You'll know how to balance your income and expenses, distinguish between assets and liabilities, set meaningful financial goals, and create a budget to manage your money effectively.

So, are you ready to take the first step towards mastering your personal finances? Let's dive into Chapter 1 and start building a strong foundation for your financial success. Stay tuned, and let's get started on this exciting path to financial literacy and independence.

Understanding the Basics

Personal finance is essentially the art and science of managing your money to achieve your financial goals and secure a stable financial future. It involves making informed decisions about earning, spending, saving, and investing. To effectively manage your personal finances, you need to grasp some key concepts. Let's break them down:

Income and Expenses

Firstly, let's talk about income. Your income is the money you earn from various sources, such as your business, investments, or employment. It's crucial to have a clear understanding of your income streams and their stability. Knowing where your money comes from helps you plan better.

Now, on to expenses. These are the costs incurred for necessities like housing, transportation, food, and utilities, as well as discretionary spending on things like entertainment and travel. Understanding your expenses and identifying areas where you can cut back on unnecessary spending is vital for achieving financial security. Think of it as balancing your financial diet: you need to nourish your financial health while avoiding the junk.

Assets and Liabilities

Next up, we have assets and liabilities. Assets are anything of value that you own, such as cash, investments, real estate, or business equity. On the flip side, liabilities are your debts or obligations, like loans, credit card balances, or mortgages. The goal here is to build a strong asset base while managing your liabilities wisely. By doing so, you achieve financial stability and create wealth over time.

Financial Goals

Setting realistic and measurable financial goals is essential for personal finance success. Your goals might include paying off debt, saving for a down payment on a property, starting a business, or building an emergency fund. By identifying your financial goals, you create a roadmap for your financial journey, helping you prioritize your actions and stay on track.

The Importance of Budgeting

Now, let's talk about budgeting. Budgeting is one of the foundational pillars of personal finance. It involves creating a detailed plan for how you'll allocate your income to meet your expenses and financial goals. A budget helps you track your spending, avoid overspending, and ensure that you're living within your means. It empowers you to make conscious decisions about your money and allocate funds to your priorities.

Tracking Your Spending

To gain control of your finances, meticulous tracking of your spending habits is essential. This includes keeping receipts, recording transactions, and categorizing expenses. By analyzing your spending patterns, you can identify areas where you can cut back and make adjustments to align your spending with your financial goals. It's like keeping a diary of your financial life, helping you understand and improve your financial habits.

Conclusion

In this chapter, we've explored the fundamentals of personal finance. Understanding the basics of income and expenses, assets and liabilities, and setting financial goals is crucial in laying the foundation for your financial success. Additionally, we've highlighted the importance of budgeting and tracking your spending as essential tools in managing your money effectively. Armed with this knowledge, you're now ready to move forward and take control of your personal finances. In the next chapter, we will dive deeper into the practical aspects of creating a personal budget.

By the end of this journey, you'll not only understand personal finance but also be able to navigate it confidently, setting yourself up for a prosperous future. So, let's continue on this path to mastering personal finance together!

Chapter 2: Creating a Personal Budget

Creating a personal budget is one of the most important steps in managing your personal finances effectively. A budget allows you to plan your income and expenses, track your spending, and make informed financial decisions. In this chapter, we will explore the key principles and steps involved in creating a personal budget.

The Importance of a Personal Budget

A personal budget serves as a roadmap for your financial journey. It helps you allocate your income efficiently, prioritize your expenses, and achieve your financial goals. With a budget in place, you have control over your money and can make informed decisions about how to spend and save. By creating a personal budget, you gain a clear understanding of your financial situation. You can identify areas where you may be overspending and make adjustments to ensure your expenses align with your income. A budget also allows you to track your progress, make necessary changes, and stay on top of your financial goals.

Steps to Create a Personal Budget

1. **Assess Your Income:** Begin by determining your total income from all

sources. This includes your salary, freelance work, passive income, and any other sources of revenue.
2. **Track Your Expenses:** Record all your expenses, both fixed and variable. Fixed expenses, such as rent or mortgage payments and utility bills, remain the same each month. Variable expenses, like groceries, entertainment, and transportation, may fluctuate.
3. **Categorize Your Expenses:** Divide your expenses into categories to gain a better understanding of your spending habits. Common categories include housing, transportation, food, entertainment, debt repayment, and savings.
4. **Prioritize Your Expenses:** Once you have categorized your expenses, prioritize them based on their importance and impact on your financial goals. Ensure essential expenses are covered first before allocating money towards discretionary spending.
5. **Set Financial Goals:** Determine your short-term and long-term financial goals. Short-term goals may include saving for a down payment on a house or paying off credit card debt. Long-term goals could involve saving for retirement or starting your own business. Your budget should reflect your goals and allocate funds accordingly.

6. **Create a Budget Plan:** Using the information gathered, create a budget plan that outlines your income, expenses, and savings goals. You can use tools such as spreadsheets, budgeting apps, or financial software to simplify the process.
7. **Review and Adjust:** Periodically review your budget to track your progress and make adjustments as needed. Evaluate your spending habits, identify areas where you can cut back, and reallocate funds to areas that align with your goals.

Tips for Successful Budgeting

- **Be Realistic:** Ensure your budget is achievable by setting realistic goals and expectations. Consider your income, expenses, and financial obligations when allocating funds.
- **Plan for Emergencies:** Include an emergency fund in your budget to cover unexpected expenses. Aim to save at least three to six months' worth of living expenses in a separate savings account.
- **Track Your Spending:** Regularly review and track your expenses to ensure you stay within your budget. Use apps or software to categorize and analyze your spending patterns.
- **Practice Self-Discipline:** Stick to your

budget and avoid unnecessary spending. Differentiate between needs and wants, and make conscious choices that align with your financial goals.
- **Seek Professional Advice if Needed:** If you find budgeting challenging or need expert guidance, consider consulting a financial advisor who can provide personalized advice and help you develop a tailored budgeting strategy.

Creating a personal budget is an essential step towards achieving financial stability and success. By gaining control over your income and expenses, you can effectively manage your money, reduce unnecessary spending, and work towards your financial goals.

Chapter 3: Managing Debt and Credit

Hey there, welcome to Chapter 3! We're diving into a crucial aspect of personal finance that every entrepreneur needs to get a handle on: managing debt and credit. This chapter is all about equipping you with the strategies to manage your debt and credit effectively, ensuring you maintain financial stability and set yourself up for long-term success.

Understanding Debt

First things first, let's talk about debt. Simply put, debt is a financial obligation you take on when you borrow money or acquire goods and services on credit. It's vital to understand the difference between good debt and bad debt.

Good debt is when you borrow for investments that are likely to appreciate in value over time, such as education or starting a business. These types of debt can potentially bring significant returns and help you grow financially. On the flip side, bad debt is excessive borrowing for non-essential items like luxury goods or vacations. This kind of debt doesn't add value and can quickly spiral out of control if not managed properly.

Evaluating Your Debt

Before we dive into managing debt, it's essential to take stock of your current situation. Start by listing all your debts. This includes credit card balances, student loans, mortgages, car loans, and any other outstanding loans you might have. For each debt, note the interest rates, minimum payments, and total balances. This comprehensive overview will help you understand where you stand and what needs attention.

Creating a Debt Repayment Strategy

Now that you have a clear picture of your debts, it's time to develop a strategy to pay them off. One effective approach is to prioritize high-interest debts first, as these can accumulate quickly and end up costing you more in the long run. Whenever possible, make more than the minimum payments to accelerate your debt payoff. This not only reduces the principal faster but also saves you money on interest over time.

Consolidating Debt

Another strategy worth considering is debt consolidation. If you have multiple debts with varying interest rates, consolidating them into a single loan with a lower interest rate can simplify your debt management and potentially save you money on interest payments. This way, you have just one payment to focus on each month, making it easier to stay on track.

Understanding Credit

Credit is another cornerstone of personal finance. It represents your ability to borrow money and is crucial for entrepreneurs, as it can determine your ability to secure loans and obtain favorable interest rates. Maintaining good credit is key to financial success.

Building Credit

If you're just starting to build your credit history, there are a few steps you can take. Consider applying for a credit card, making regular payments, and keeping your credit utilization ratio low. Paying bills on time, such as rent and utilities, also contributes to building a positive credit history. The goal is to demonstrate responsible borrowing and repayment habits.

Maintaining Good Credit

To maintain a good credit score, consistency is key. Make payments on time and avoid accumulating too much debt. Keep your credit utilization ratio below 30%, meaning you should only use up to 30% of your available credit. Regularly review your credit reports to ensure accuracy and promptly address any errors.

Managing Credit Wisely

While credit can be a powerful tool, it's important to use it wisely. Avoid unnecessary borrowing and only use credit when it's necessary. Be cautious of credit card debt, as high-interest rates can quickly add up. Develop healthy financial habits like budgeting and saving to reduce your reliance on credit. These practices will help you manage your credit more effectively and avoid potential pitfalls.

Conclusion

Effectively managing debt and credit is vital for entrepreneurs aiming for financial stability and success. By understanding debt, evaluating your situation, and implementing strategies such as debt repayment and wise credit management, you can take control of your financial future. Remember, managing debt and credit requires discipline and responsible decision-making. Stay proactive, and you'll pave the way to a brighter, more secure financial future.

Keep reading to uncover valuable insights on saving and emergency funds in Chapter 4: Saving and Emergency Funds. Let's continue this journey to mastering your personal finance!

Chapter 4: Understanding the Importance of Saving and Emergency Funds

Saving money is a cornerstone of personal finance. It's the key to building a financial safety net, achieving long-term financial goals, and maintaining peace of mind during unexpected events. In this chapter, we'll explore the many benefits of saving and guide you through the steps to establish a robust emergency fund.

The Benefits of Saving

There are numerous advantages to saving money, and understanding these can motivate you to prioritize saving in your financial plan.

1. **Financial Security:** Having savings provides a safety net that protects you from unexpected expenses or financial hardships. With savings, you can handle emergencies without resorting to loans or credit cards, which can lead to debt.
2. **Achieving Financial Goals:** Saving enables you to work towards your financial goals, whether it's buying a house, starting a business, or taking a

dream vacation. It provides the necessary funds to turn your aspirations into reality.
3. **Peace of Mind:** Knowing that you have money set aside gives you peace of mind. It reduces financial stress and allows you to focus on other aspects of your life and work.

Building an Emergency Fund

An emergency fund is an essential component of any financial plan. It acts as a financial cushion during unexpected events, such as medical emergencies, car repairs, or job loss. Here's how you can build an effective emergency fund:

1. **Set a Target:** Aim to save at least three to six months' worth of living expenses. This amount will provide a safety net in case of job loss or other financial difficulties.
2. **Track Your Expenses:** Assess your current spending habits and identify areas where you can cut back or reduce unnecessary expenses. This will free up more money for saving.
3. **Automate Savings:** Set up an automatic transfer from your checking account to a separate savings account. Treat this transfer as a monthly expense and prioritize it.

4. **Start Small and Increase:** If saving a significant amount seems challenging, begin with smaller monthly contributions and gradually increase the amount over time. The key is consistency.
5. **Reduce Debt:** Paying off high-interest debts, such as credit card balances, should be a priority. The interest saved can contribute towards building your emergency fund.
6. **Make Smart Financial Choices:** Evaluate your current financial commitments and identify areas where you can reduce expenses. Consider options such as downsizing your home or cutting back on unnecessary subscriptions.

Maximizing Your Savings

While building an emergency fund is crucial, it's also important to maximize your savings to meet long-term financial goals. Here are a few strategies to achieve this:

1. **Reduce Expenses:** Review your monthly expenses and identify areas where you can cut back or negotiate better deals. Every dollar saved can contribute towards your savings.
2. **Increase Income:** Explore opportunities to boost your income, such as taking on

a side hustle, freelancing, or investing in assets that generate passive income.
3. **Invest Wisely:** Consider investing your savings in assets that offer higher returns, such as stocks, bonds, or real estate. However, ensure you have a good understanding of the risks and seek professional advice if needed.
4. **Keep Reviewing and Adjusting:** As your financial situation changes and your goals evolve, regularly review your savings plan and make necessary adjustments. This will ensure that your savings align with your financial objectives.

Conclusion

Saving money and having an emergency fund are vital aspects of personal finance. They provide financial security, allow for the achievement of long-term goals, and offer peace of mind during unexpected events. By following the steps outlined in this chapter and making conscious financial choices, you will be well on your way to mastering personal finance and securing a prosperous future. Remember, the journey of a thousand miles begins with a single step, so start saving today and build the foundation for a financially stable tomorrow.

Chapter 5: Investing for the Future

Investing is a cornerstone of personal finance that empowers individuals to grow their wealth and achieve long-term financial goals. For entrepreneurs, investing wisely can make your money work for you, ensuring a prosperous future. In this chapter, we'll delve into the world of investing, exploring various strategies and key considerations for successful investments.

The Importance of Investing

Investing isn't just about putting your money into stocks or real estate; it's about strategically allocating your resources to generate returns that outpace inflation and help you build wealth over time. Here are some compelling reasons why investing is essential for entrepreneurs:

1. **Wealth Accumulation:** Investing allows you to grow your money and accumulate wealth. Instead of solely relying on your income, investments offer the potential for your assets to appreciate and generate additional income.
2. **Financial Independence:** Investing can pave the way to financial freedom. By building a strong investment portfolio, you can create a passive income stream that supports your desired lifestyle

without being dependent on actively working.
3. **Beating Inflation:** Inflation erodes the purchasing power of money over time. By investing, you have the opportunity to earn returns that surpass the inflation rate, enabling you to maintain your purchasing power and preserve the value of your wealth.
4. **Early Retirement:** Investing early and consistently can accelerate your journey to financial independence and early retirement. By generating passive income through investments, you can potentially retire earlier and enjoy the fruits of your labor.

Understanding Different Investment Options

Before diving into investing, it's crucial to understand the various options available. Here are some common investment choices entrepreneurs can consider:

1. **Stocks:** Investing in individual stocks allows you to become a partial owner of a company. Stocks can offer significant capital appreciation potential, but they also come with risks. It's important to conduct thorough research and diversify your stock portfolio.
2. **Bonds:** Bonds are debt securities

issued by governments or corporations. Investing in bonds means lending money to the issuer in exchange for regular interest payments and the return of the principal amount at maturity. Bonds are generally considered less risky than stocks.
3. **Mutual Funds:** Mutual funds pool money from multiple investors to invest in a diversified portfolio of stocks, bonds, or other assets. Managed by professional fund managers, mutual funds offer diversification and convenience for investors.
4. **Real Estate:** Investing in real estate involves purchasing properties for rental income or capital appreciation. Real estate can provide stable cash flow and act as a hedge against inflation, but it requires careful analysis, management, and maintenance.
5. **Exchange-Traded Funds (ETFs):** ETFs are similar to mutual funds but trade on stock exchanges like individual stocks. They offer diversification and liquidity, making them an attractive option for many investors.

Developing an Investment Strategy

Building a successful investment strategy involves careful planning and consideration of your financial goals, risk tolerance, and time horizon. Here are some steps to help you develop a sound investment strategy:

1. **Set Clear Financial Goals:** Define your short-term and long-term financial goals. Are you investing for retirement, buying a house, or funding your children's education? Setting clear goals will help you determine the appropriate investment approach.
2. **Assess Risk Tolerance:** Evaluate your willingness and ability to take on investment risks. Consider factors such as your age, financial stability, and investment knowledge. Understanding your risk tolerance will help you choose investments that align with your comfort level.
3. **Diversify Your Portfolio:** Diversification is key to reducing investment risk. Spread your investments across different asset classes, industries, and geographic regions. This helps minimize the impact of a single investment's performance on your overall portfolio.
4. **Stay Informed:** Keep up-to-date with the latest financial news, market trends, and economic developments. Staying informed about the performance of your investments will help you make necessary adjustments and stay on track.
5. **Monitor and Rebalance:** Regularly

review your investment portfolio and make necessary adjustments to ensure it aligns with your goals and risk tolerance. Rebalancing involves adjusting the proportions of different investments to maintain the desired asset allocation.

Conclusion

Investing for the future is a critical component of personal finance for entrepreneurs. By understanding the importance of investing, exploring different investment options, and developing a sound investment strategy, you can take control of your financial future and work towards achieving long-term success. Remember, investing involves risks, so it's essential to educate yourself and seek professional advice when needed.

Now that you have a solid understanding of investing, let's move on to the next chapter, where we will explore the topic of retirement planning.

Chapter 6: Retirement Planning

Retirement planning is one of those crucial aspects of personal finance that often gets overlooked, especially by entrepreneurs. It's understandable—building a successful business can be all-consuming. However, neglecting your retirement planning can lead to serious consequences down the road. So, let's dive into why retirement planning is essential and how you can get started.

Why Retirement Planning is Important

First things first, why should you care about retirement planning? Here are a few key reasons:

1. **Maintaining Your Lifestyle:** Retirement planning helps ensure that you can maintain your current standard of living and financial independence once you stop working. Without a solid plan, you might find yourself struggling financially or depending solely on government programs, which might not be sufficient.
2. **Financial Security and Peace of Mind:** Having a dedicated retirement plan provides a sense of security. Knowing that you have a strategy in place to

support you in your later years can alleviate a lot of stress about your financial future.
3. **Achieving Your Desired Lifestyle:** Retirement isn't just about not working; it's about enjoying life. Whether you want to travel, pick up new hobbies, or spend more time with family, a well-thought-out retirement plan gives you the financial freedom to pursue these goals.

Considerations for Retirement Planning

When you start thinking about retirement planning, there are several key factors to consider. Let's break them down:

1. Start Early

The earlier you start planning for retirement, the better. Time is your greatest ally because of the power of compounding. Starting early means your investments have more time to grow and multiply, significantly increasing your retirement savings over the years.

2. Determine Retirement Goals

Before you can create a retirement plan, you need to know what you're aiming for. Ask yourself questions like: When do I want to retire? What kind of lifestyle do I want? What are my expected expenses? Having clear goals will guide your saving and investment strategies.

3. Estimate Retirement Expenses

It's crucial to have a realistic estimate of your future retirement expenses. Think about housing, healthcare, transportation, and leisure activities. Don't forget to factor in inflation and potential healthcare costs, which can be significant.

4. Assess Retirement Income Sources

Look at the various sources of income you'll have during retirement. This might include savings, investments, social security benefits, and any pension plans. Understanding your potential income streams will help you identify any gaps that need to be filled.

5. Develop a Savings Strategy

Based on your retirement goals and estimated expenses, develop a savings strategy. Consider setting up automatic contributions to retirement accounts like an Individual Retirement Account (IRA) or a 401(k). Try to maximize your contributions to take advantage of tax benefits and any employer matches.

6. Diversify Investments

Diversification is key to a robust retirement plan. Spread your investments across different asset classes such as stocks, bonds, and real estate. This helps mitigate risk and maximize returns, protecting your savings from market volatility and economic downturns.

7. Regularly Review and Adjust

Retirement planning isn't a set-it-and-forget-it activity. It's important to regularly review and adjust your plan based on changes in your circumstances and market conditions. Revisit your goals, reassess your risk tolerance, and make necessary adjustments to your investment portfolio.

Conclusion

Retirement planning is a vital component of personal finance, especially for entrepreneurs. By starting early, setting clear goals, estimating expenses, assessing income sources, developing a savings strategy, diversifying investments, and regularly reviewing and adjusting your plan, you can take proactive steps towards a financially secure retirement. Don't overlook the importance of retirement planning; it's an investment in your future and your financial well-being. Take the time now to ensure you can enjoy the fruits of your labor when it's time to retire.

Chapter 7: Insurance and Risk Management

Hey there, welcome to Chapter 7! In this chapter, we're going to talk about insurance and risk management, two vital components of personal finance that every entrepreneur should understand. These tools help protect you against financial risks and potential losses, ensuring that both your business and personal assets are safeguarded. Let's dive into the different types of insurance coverage you should consider and explore strategies for managing risks effectively.

Understanding Insurance

Insurance is essentially a contract between you (the insured) and an insurance company. In this agreement, you pay regular premiums, and in return, the insurance company provides financial protection against potential losses. Think of insurance as a safety net that helps cushion the financial blow of unexpected events, such as accidents, natural disasters, or even lawsuits.

Here are some common types of insurance coverage that entrepreneurs should definitely consider:

Health Insurance

1. Health insurance is crucial because it covers medical expenses, including doctor visits, hospitalization, and medications. As an entrepreneur, it's essential to have health insurance to protect yourself and your family from the high costs of healthcare. You can look into various options, such as employer-sponsored plans, private insurance, or government programs like Medicaid.

Property Insurance

2. Property insurance protects your business and personal assets, like buildings, equipment, and inventory, against damage or loss from fire, theft, vandalism, or natural disasters. It's important to accurately assess the value of your assets and choose appropriate coverage limits to ensure you're adequately protected.

Liability Insurance

3. Liability insurance shields you and your business from claims and lawsuits filed by third parties for bodily injury, property damage, or negligence. For entrepreneurs, having liability insurance

is essential to protect against potential financial losses from legal disputes.

Business Interruption Insurance

4. Business interruption insurance provides coverage for lost income and expenses if your business operations are disrupted due to factors beyond your control, such as a fire, natural disaster, or other unforeseen events. This type of insurance can help you recover financially and resume your business operations as quickly as possible.

Professional Liability Insurance

5. Also known as errors and omissions insurance, professional liability insurance is crucial for entrepreneurs who provide professional services or advice. It protects against claims of negligence, errors, or omissions that may arise from your professional activities. This coverage can save your business from significant financial losses resulting from lawsuits or damages.

Risk Management Strategies
In addition to having the right insurance, it's

essential to implement effective risk management strategies. Here are some strategies to consider:

Identify and Assess Risks

1. Start by identifying potential risks that may affect your business. This could include risks related to operations, market fluctuations, legal and regulatory compliance, and cybersecurity. Assess the likelihood and impact of each risk and develop strategies to mitigate or avoid them.

Implement Risk Control Measures

2. Take steps to minimize the likelihood or impact of risks. This might involve implementing safety protocols, regular maintenance of equipment, cybersecurity measures, and ensuring compliance with relevant laws and regulations.

Develop a Business Continuity Plan

3. Create a business continuity plan that outlines the steps to take in the event of a disruption or crisis. This plan should include procedures for communication,

employee safety, data backup, and alternative business operations. Regularly review and update the plan as needed.

Diversify Your Business and Investments

4. Diversification involves spreading out your business activities and investments across different sectors or industries. This helps reduce the impact of a potential loss in one area by having other areas that may still generate income. Diversifying your business and investments can protect you from concentration risk.

Stay Informed and Seek Professional Advice

5. Keep yourself updated about industry trends, changes in regulations, and emerging risks that may impact your business. Consider seeking professional advice from insurance brokers, financial advisors, and legal counsel to ensure you have the right coverage and risk management strategies in place.

Conclusion

Insurance and risk management are crucial for protecting entrepreneurs and their businesses from unexpected events and potential financial losses. By understanding different insurance coverage options and implementing effective risk management strategies, you can safeguard your assets, minimize financial risks, and focus on long-term business success. Don't underestimate the importance of these tools in securing your financial future as an entrepreneur.

Keep reading to discover valuable insights on saving and emergency funds in Chapter 8: Saving and Emergency Funds. Let's continue this journey to mastering your personal finance!

Chapter 8: Tax Planning and Optimization

Taxes are a fact of life, especially for entrepreneurs. Understanding how to manage and optimize your tax situation is essential for ensuring you don't pay more than you have to while staying on the right side of the law. In this chapter, we'll delve into valuable insights and strategies to help you minimize your tax liability effectively.

Understanding the Basics of Taxation

Before diving into the nitty-gritty of tax planning strategies, it's crucial to grasp the different types of taxes that entrepreneurs may face. Here are some key concepts to familiarize yourself with:

Income Taxes

Income taxes are levied on the income earned by both individuals and businesses. As an entrepreneur, you'll be responsible for paying income tax on the profits generated by your business. It's vital to accurately track and report your income to ensure compliance with tax laws.

Capital Gains Taxes

Capital gains taxes apply to the profit realized from selling assets such as stocks, bonds, real estate, or even your business. If you make investments or decide to sell your business, you'll need to calculate and pay capital gains taxes on the profits.

Deductions and Credits
Deductions and credits are powerful tools to help reduce your tax liability. Deductions allow you to subtract certain expenses from your taxable income, while credits provide a dollar-for-dollar reduction in the amount of tax you owe. Familiarizing yourself with these can significantly lower your tax bill.

Developing a Tax Planning Strategy
A well-thought-out tax planning strategy can minimize your tax burden and maximize your financial resources. Here are some key steps to consider when developing your tax plan:

Evaluate Your Business Structure
The legal structure of your business can significantly impact your tax obligations. Whether you operate as a sole proprietor, partnership, LLC, or corporation, understanding the tax advantages and disadvantages associated with each structure is crucial. Consulting with a tax professional can help you determine the most tax-efficient structure for your business.

Know Your Deductions and Credits
Take the time to familiarize yourself with the deductions and credits available to you as an entrepreneur. Common deductions include business-related expenses such as office rent,

equipment, travel, and marketing costs. Research and identify any industry-specific deductions or credits that may apply to your business.

Keep Accurate Records and Separate Personal from Business Expenses
Maintaining clear and accurate financial records is essential for effective tax planning. Keeping personal and business expenses separate not only simplifies record-keeping but also ensures you can claim all eligible deductions and credits related to your business.

Consider Tax-Advantaged Retirement Accounts
Entrepreneurs can take advantage of various tax-advantaged retirement accounts to save for their future while reducing their taxable income. Some options include SEP IRAs, SIMPLE IRAs, and solo 401(k) plans. These accounts offer tax benefits, such as tax-deductible contributions or tax-free growth, depending on the type of account.

Strategically Time Income and Expenses
Carefully timing your income and expenses can help optimize your tax situation. For example, if you anticipate a higher income in the following year, you may want to defer some income or accelerate deductible expenses into the current year to lower your tax liability.

Consult with a Tax Professional

Navigating the complexities of tax planning and optimization can be challenging for entrepreneurs. Seeking professional advice from a tax accountant or financial planner who specializes in working with entrepreneurs can help you develop a comprehensive tax plan tailored to your unique circumstances.

Staying Informed and Adapting to Tax Changes
Tax laws and regulations are subject to change, so it's essential to stay informed and adapt your tax planning strategies accordingly. Regularly review updates from the tax authorities and consult with professionals to ensure that you are incorporating the most current tax laws into your planning.

Monitor Your Tax Plan Regularly
Maintaining a proactive approach to tax planning involves periodically reviewing and adjusting your tax plan. Changes in your business, income level, or tax laws may necessitate modifications to your strategies. By staying attentive and making necessary changes, you can continue to optimize your tax situation and maximize your financial resources.

Conclusion
Tax planning and optimization are critical components of personal finance for entrepreneurs. By understanding the basics of taxation, developing a strategic tax plan, and

staying informed about changes in tax laws, you can minimize your tax liability and make the most of your financial resources. Remember, consulting with a tax professional is always a wise investment to ensure compliance and maximize your tax savings. With careful planning and the right strategies, you can navigate the complexities of taxes and keep more of your hard-earned money.

Chapter 9: Estate Planning and Wealth Transfer

Hey there, welcome to Chapter 9! We're going to talk about estate planning and wealth transfer, which are essential topics for entrepreneurs, especially those with significant assets and wealth. Estate planning involves making decisions about how to distribute your assets and resources to your loved ones after you pass away. It ensures your wishes are carried out, minimizes estate taxes, and provides financial security for future generations.

The Importance of Estate Planning

Estate planning is crucial for entrepreneurs for several reasons:

1. **Smooth Wealth Transfer**

Estate planning allows you to ensure a smooth transfer of your wealth to your chosen beneficiaries. Without an estate plan, your assets may be distributed in ways that don't align with your wishes or could become subject to legal disputes. By creating a comprehensive plan, you can designate exactly how your assets should be distributed and to whom.

2. **Minimize Taxes**

Estate taxes can significantly reduce the amount of wealth transferred to your beneficiaries. However, with proper planning, you can minimize the impact of these taxes on your estate. This might involve establishing trusts, implementing gifting strategies, or utilizing other tax-saving techniques. Seeking guidance from a professional estate planner or attorney can provide valuable insights into minimizing your tax liability.

3. Protecting Your Loved Ones

Estate planning helps you protect your loved ones, ensuring their financial security even after you're gone. You can establish trusts to provide for ongoing needs, such as education expenses, healthcare costs, or general living expenses. By implementing a comprehensive estate plan, you can offer peace of mind to your loved ones and safeguard their financial well-being.

4. Business Succession

For entrepreneurs, estate planning is closely tied to business succession planning. If you own a business, it's crucial to consider how it will be transferred or managed after your passing. Through proper estate planning, you can outline your wishes for the business's future, designate a successor, and establish a plan for a smooth transition of ownership. This helps protect the continuity and long-term success of your business.

Key Components of Estate Planning

When creating an estate plan, there are several key components to consider:

1. Will

A will is a legally binding document that outlines how your assets should be distributed after your death. It allows you to designate beneficiaries, specify asset distributions, appoint guardians for minor children, and name an executor to handle the distribution process. Creating a will is essential to ensure your wishes are followed and to minimize potential disputes among your heirs.

2. Trusts

Trusts are legal arrangements that can hold and manage your assets for the benefit of your beneficiaries. There are various types of trusts, including revocable living trusts, irrevocable trusts, and charitable trusts. Trusts offer advantages such as avoiding probate, providing ongoing management of assets, and protecting assets from certain creditors.

Consulting with an estate planning attorney or financial advisor can help you determine the most suitable trust structure for your needs.

3. Power of Attorney

A power of attorney allows you to appoint someone to make financial or legal decisions on your behalf if you become incapacitated. This ensures that your financial affairs are managed effectively and according to your wishes, even if you are unable to do so yourself. Choosing a trustworthy and capable individual to act as your power of attorney is crucial.

4. Advanced Healthcare Directive

An advanced healthcare directive (also known as a living will or healthcare proxy) outlines your wishes regarding medical treatment and end-of-life care. It allows you to specify the medical interventions you want or do not want in certain circumstances. This document ensures that your healthcare decisions align with your values and beliefs, even if you are unable to communicate them.

Working with Professionals

Creating a comprehensive estate plan can be complex, so it's recommended to seek guidance from professionals with expertise in estate planning and wealth transfer. These professionals may include estate planning attorneys, financial advisors, and tax specialists. They can help ensure that your plan aligns with your goals, maximizes tax efficiency, and navigates any legal complexities.

Regular Review and Updating

Estate planning isn't a one-time activity. It's essential to regularly review and update your plan as circumstances change. Life events such as marriage, divorce, births, deaths, changes in financial circumstances, or modifications to tax laws may necessitate revisions to your estate plan. Regularly consulting with your financial and legal advisors will help ensure your plan remains relevant and effective.

Conclusion

Estate planning and wealth transfer are vital components of personal finance for entrepreneurs. By creating a comprehensive estate plan, you can protect your loved ones, ensure the smooth transfer of assets, minimize tax liabilities, and secure the future of your business. Working with professionals and regularly reviewing your plan will help ensure your wishes are carried out and your financial legacy is preserved.

Let's continue this journey together and delve into the next important topic in personal finance. Keep reading to equip yourself with all the knowledge you need to secure a prosperous future.

Chapter 10: Continuously Improving and Monitoring Your Financial Health

As an entrepreneur, it's not enough to just create a personal budget, manage debt, save, invest, plan for retirement, and have insurance and estate plans in place. It's equally important to continuously improve and monitor your financial health. This chapter delves into why ongoing financial management is crucial and provides actionable tips to help you continuously enhance your financial well-being.

Why is Continuously Improving and Monitoring Your Financial Health Important?

Financial health isn't a destination; it's a lifelong journey. As an entrepreneur, your financial situation will constantly evolve with your business growth, market changes, and personal life shifts. Continuously improving and monitoring your financial health is essential for several reasons:

1. Identifying Areas of Improvement
Regularly reviewing your finances helps you pinpoint areas where adjustments can improve your financial well-being. This might include finding ways to reduce expenses, increase savings, optimize investments, or streamline

your tax strategy.

2. Adapting to Changing Circumstances
Life is unpredictable. As an entrepreneur, you might face unexpected events or changes in your personal or business life. By continuously monitoring your financial health, you can adapt your plans and strategies accordingly. For instance, if your income fluctuates, you may need to adjust your budget or savings targets.

3. Measuring Progress
Tracking your financial progress is crucial for staying motivated and focused on your long-term goals. Regularly monitoring your financial health allows you to see how far you've come and celebrate your achievements. It also helps you stay accountable and make necessary course corrections.

Tips for Continuously Improving and Monitoring Your Financial Health

Here are some practical tips to help you keep improving and monitoring your financial health:

1. Review Your Budget Regularly
A budget isn't a one-time exercise; it's an ongoing process. Review your budget monthly or quarterly to ensure it still aligns with your financial goals and reflects any changes in your income or expenses. Look for areas where you can cut back or reallocate funds to

support your priorities.

2. Track Your Spending
Monitoring your expenses is crucial for financial success. Use tools or apps to track your spending and categorize your expenses. This will help you identify areas where you may be overspending and make informed decisions about where to allocate your money.

3. Reassess Your Debt Strategy
If you have outstanding debts, regularly evaluate your debt strategy to ensure it aligns with your financial goals. Consider refinancing or consolidating your debts to save on interest payments. Reassess your repayment plan and aim to pay off high-interest debts first.

4. Monitor Investment Performance
Keep a close eye on your investment portfolio's performance. Review your investments regularly to ensure they align with your risk tolerance and long-term goals. Consider rebalancing your portfolio if necessary or seeking advice from a financial advisor.

5. Stay Informed
The world of personal finance is constantly evolving. Stay up-to-date with financial news and changes in laws or regulations that may affect your financial situation. This will help you make informed decisions and adapt your strategies accordingly.

6. Regularly Update Your Insurance Coverage

As your business and personal circumstances change, reassess your insurance needs. Ensure your coverage adequately protects you against potential risks and liabilities. Consult with an insurance professional to ensure you have the right policies in place.

7. Review and Update Estate Plans

Life events, such as marriage, divorce, or the birth of children, may require updates to your estate plans. Regularly review your will, trusts, and other estate planning documents to ensure they reflect your current wishes and distribute your assets as intended.

8. Seek Professional Advice

If you feel overwhelmed or unsure about certain aspects of your financial management, don't hesitate to seek professional advice. Financial advisors, accountants, and tax experts can provide valuable guidance tailored to your specific situation.

Conclusion

Continuously improving and monitoring your financial health is an integral part of personal finance for entrepreneurs. By regularly reviewing your financial situation and adapting your plans and strategies, you can ensure that you stay on track toward your long-term goals. Remember, financial health is a lifelong journey, so embrace the process of continuous improvement and enjoy the rewards it brings.

www.ingramcontent.com/pod-product-compliance
Lightning Source LLC
Chambersburg PA
CBHW050245230526
45470CB00005B/2121